an anthology to

foraging

love in the forest of fiction and fakeness

GLOBALAGE POETRY

Poetry for ages

Foraging

India. Singapore. Malaysia.

ISBN 978-93-5321-160-8

First Published and printed in India by
Globalage Poetry, August 2018
MC Nicholas Road, Chetpet, Chennai, Tamil Nadu 600031

Administration Office: Purva Corner, Baramati (413102) , Pune,
Maharashtra ,India.

GLOBALAGE POETRY

The book is dedicated to all the writers and their parents
Illustration art by:
Sanda- Instagram (@broken_isnt_bad)

Contents

Foreword

FORAGING is the debut poetry collection by the Instagram global platform, Globalage Poetry. It is a collection of poetry and prose about love in this modern world with a hint of problems in our society.

The word "foraging" means a search which implies a search of love in this cosmopolitan world of fakeness and fiction, about the experience of violence, abuse, love, loss, sociality, manhood and femininity. The book is a collective effort of a number of writers and poets of which each piece serves different purpose of healing. This is to heal a different heartache that everyone constantly holds. Foraging is sure to bring inner happiness to all those with some sort of pain.

Moreover under collective efforts of GLOBALAGE POETRY we are constantly trying to bring those beautiful hidden poets and writers on stage by providing a platform through our free publishing, E-zine press and featuring through our Instagram pages. This exquisite and thought provoking book features poems, micro tales, interviews and prose from 110 of the most talented, popular and exciting new voices on Instagram today..

This book is a collection of wonderful write-ups by a number of writers and poets from around world.

Here every piece has been selected with absolute care. The book has been curated by Editors Ajay Sawant , Niksha Nath and Associate Editors Varun Sharma and Nomi Murumi who are based in India. The book aims towards building future for poetry in this vibrant area of internet. Our only motto is to make poetry live for ages...

Ajay Sawant

Founder Globalage Poetry

Date 10th July 2018

Preface

Poetry writing and reading has become the "need of the day" in today's world. Where it was actually supposed to be degraded by today it has become a real trend in writers and life of common people to relieve them from the daily stress they are going through. Poetry reading and writing is an exercise to gauge command of language skill and it's uses.

In this book which has been presented in front of you with involvence of numerous poets and writers, all the beautiful concepts on love and likely topics have been elaborated which 'll surely get you into fancy.

Author name Ms. Iris Castillo

Date 2nd August 2018

Acknowledgments

This book has been curated by:

Ajay Sawant
(Founder and Editor-in-chief
Globalage Poetry)

Niksha Nath
(Editor-in-chief Globalage Poetry)

The following book includes the contributions of numerous poets and writers. The names and instagram usernames of these wonderful supertalents is mentioned below :

1) Gaurav Dubey (@the_unwanted_heart_feelings)
2) Heini Talip (@missfinnpoet)
3) Aryan Lohia (@aryan._.lohia23)
4) Liza Monin (@ecstacsy_in_words)
5) Mrinalini Sarkar (@imrinalini)
6) Nischita Nibedita (@nischitanivedita)
7) Deblina Bhattacharya (@author_deblina)
8) Ashleigh Rayl (@ashrayl)
9) Ayema Faisal (@poetesstic)
10) Anoop Kumar Sureka (@_i_m_anoop_)
11) Chitrapu Ravali (@ravalisonu)
12) Akeel Bhat (@akeelbhat)
13) Deepesh Katariya (@the_irksome_admirer)
14) Kavya Rajendran (@kavyaraja98)
15) Gopika Menon (@your.poetrygirl_)
16) Arati Khanal (@house_of_prose_and_poetry)
17) Pritha Bose (@_the_colonel)
18) Fahima Nizar (@fahima_nizar)
19) AK Stars Above (@whispersofbrokenheart)
20) Agnes Belen Operiano (@dec_embre)
21) Gursimar Kaur (@pen_fight)
22) Shreyashi Deb (@__bubble_boo__)
23) Astha Vyas (@vyas_astha)
24) Brin Battisti (@_mybeautifulchaos___)
25) Dhiman Saha (@poetryofdhiman)
26) Shruti Agrawal (@writershruti)
27) Nistha Goel (@_alikeu_)
28) Allegra Minerva (@a.m.doespoems)
29) Khushbu Patel (@_khushi_writes)
30) Preeta Roy (@in.the.autumn.of.words)
31) Myra Dutta (@fairies_and_lust)

32) Harshal Bajaj (@harshlbajaj06)
33) Jahnvi Raol (@untold._.feels)
34) Disha Dahiya (@disha.writes)
35) Saumya Singh (@saumyeah)
36) Riya Nagpal (@serene_purpose)
37) Aboli Mane (@writer_abby)
38) Prashant Pundir (@aliterarysoul)
39) Ayushi Jain (@ayushi_sancheti)
40) Ishita srivastava (@ish_writings)
41) Ratnadeep Acharya (@writes._._deep)
42) Disha Mohanty (@__lost._.wanderer__)
43) Rohit Das (@guchupoofficial)
44) Shreya Gupta (@_creouscule__)
45) Guru (@__it_wasnt_me____)
46) Soniya S (@feelings_awestruck)
47) Srishti (the_bleeding_pen._)
48) Shweta Gautam (@_loveforwords_)
49) Shamita Singh (@amyra_19)
50) Lesley Worthington (@worthywrites)
51) Ami Johri (@26_amisba)
52) Khushboo Jain (@khush0133)
53) Fiza Farheen (@its_her_thought)
54) Roopi (@wordsworld_life)
55) Rachitha M. R. (@17_rach)
56) Aisha Shaikh (@aishashaikh121)
57) Niksha Nath (@niksha_justanamateur)
58) Ajay Sawant (@rumiet.ry)
59) Anna Cherian (@sparklesandink)
60) Payal Hora (@the_comely_ingenue)
61) Niva Kalita (@feelings_voiced)
62) Somya Thakur (@sammiediaries)
63) Bk Murumi (@bkmurumi)
64) Rawan Ameer (@poetic_author)
65) Rosalie Pantzalis (@sserpfl_rn4l)
66) Lyn Patterson (@poetryntings)
67) Shivanshi Pandey (@whiskpoetry)

68) Isha Singh (@shhitsish)
69) Subhajit Sahoo (@subhajits_diary)
70) Jules Stevenson (@j.s.poet)
71) Sheetal Bhatta (@letters_inc)
72) Shambhavi Singh (@khichdi_in_shampagne)
73) Olatunde Brain (@brain7days)
74) Vivienne Yu (@wordsbyhuman)
75) Sahana Kumar (@sahana_kruti)
76) Aafreen Ahmed (@i.soulfulgirl)
77) Andaleeb Qureshi (@night_in_gale.writings)
78) Dyan Bowers (@grahmcrackergirl)
79) Gayle Dmello (@ just_a_girl_with_words)
80) Divyanshu Giri (@poetryby.d)
81) Vanashree Yadav Gautam (@vignettes_by_v)
82) Dhanlaxmi Kumaresan (@penning_down_my_thoughts)
83) George Gumikiriza (@sir_wootridge.writes)
84) Kyla Newman (@thewritingloft)
85) Oderuth Oozeer Mehneez (@dreamy.words)
86) Varun Sharma (@vs.writes)
87) Aanchal Rout (@27.91del)
88) Elizabeth Brady (@lightofmylifefireofmyloin5)
89) Jayme Smith (@jlsmith_odist)
90) Asmita Mohanty (@asmitaamohantyy)
91) Edwin John A (@e.j.tulik)
92) Norah Arriya (@ruminatingsoul)
93) Cheyenne Tyler Jacobs (@shewillspeak)
94) Arpit Jain (@your_alter_ego)
95) Barsha Kunda (@the_quotes_cafe)
96) Sneha Wasan (@snehawassan)
97) Akshay Joshi (@mr.thronex)
98) Aishwarya Rudrappa (@aishwarya.rudrappa.writes)
99) Khadija Inam (@k.inam_)
100) Cassandra Wood (@cm.writer)
101) Moiz Mahabaleshwarwala (@quilleddiaries)

102) Aakash Kumar Nanda (@aakash_kumar_5)
103) Anasuya Bardhan (@hridmajhhare)
104) Niyanta Sailor (@s.niyanta)
105) Divyanshi Mishra (@wildpoetria)
106) Ravisha Singh (@muserofhearts)
107) Maseera (@maseera.arif)
108) Tushar Ranjan Behera (@the_eloquent_philosopher)
109) Ajay Savant(@ajaysavant____)
110) Sahla (@mystical_hues)

The pages that you read unfold the efforts of numerous writers. The book you are reading has been shaped by a number of writers. We would like to thank and praise our entire team of GLOBALAGE POETRY who work day and night encouraging writers by featuring them namely

Niksha Nath (@niksha_justanamateur)
Ajay Sawant (@rumiet.ry)
Varun Sharma (@vs.writes)
Khadija Inam (@k.inam_)
Shivanshi Pandey (@whiskpoetry)
Isha Singh (@shhitsish)
Cassandra Wood (@cm.writer)
Subhajit Sahoo (@subhajits_diary)
Jules Stevenson (@j.s.poet)
Nomi Murumi (@bkmurumi)
Shweta Gautam (@_loveforwords_)
Divya Robinson (@thebleedingquill)
Chey (@shewillspeak)
Alexis (@_astoldbylex)

Moreover we would also like to thank all the co writers for contributing.
Thanks a bunch !

A special thanks to Sanda (@broken_isnt_bad) for letting us use her beautiful illustrations.

Writeups on foraging

"Foraging for love was a semicolon to me;

A pause, but not a full stop,
When you and I decided never to cross paths,
Until raindrops start to catch fire or we inhale
sadness in one draught."

~Team Globalage Poetry
Varun Sharma
(Team Member and H.C Globalage Caption)

Foraging for love was like searching for illustrations in a fiction book
it just faked.

~Ajay Sawant
@rumiet.ry

Foraging for love was a journey to remember.
It did not take me places, but it brought me closer to my soul.

~Shambhavi Singh
@khichdi_in_shampagne

I travelled through the oceans,
Toiling the woods, finding good luck and happiness ,
I got stabbed but I never stopped running ,
Blood flows through my eyes and my cold skin cry for hugs,
This is me foraging for your love.

~Olatunde Brain
@brain7days

Love among the carnivores—
Frivol, haphazard, endless squandering ,
A group of savages, foraging for love,
Was—desperate and primal ,
With an unyielding appetite,
Preying to satisfy their abysmal desires.

~Vivienne Yu
@wordsbyhuman

Foraging for Love of the Great Ancestors to be blessed upon the cards Fate dealt me with, I had to stop dead in my tracks to realize that I too, could be history, written down with a force that compelled the youth to inspire love in the world, rather than go foraging for it all in the blind hypnosis of ancient beliefs, that will forever remain dead.

~Sahla,
@mystical_hues

Foraging for love,
Was wandering,
And awaiting,
To be loved at,
Each place where,
I lost fragments of myself,
But suddenly realizing,
I was just a mirror away,
To find the love,
Of My Life.

~Andaleeb Qureshi
@night_in_gale.writings

Foraging for love,
That's how it was,
Trenches and fences,
Sideline benches,
An empty basket filled with wishes or,
Pale moon traces and frontline glimpses.

~Dyan Bowers
@grahmcrackergirl

Foraging for love was like seeking embers of my soul
amidst the forest fires.
It was a quest unlonged for.

~Divyanshu Giri
@poetryby.d

Foraging for love was the quest of a lifetime and each time it ended in flames, she rose up from the ashes like a phoenix... ready to search for love again.

~ Gayle Dmello
@ just_a_girl_with_words

Foraging for love was everything similar to
walking on burning ashes of my own desires,
where I kept moving forward inspite of being aware
about the destruction it will bring for me.
Foraging for love was everything similar to
walking on nails to leave my feet bleeding,
where I kept moving forward inspite of being aware
about the torment it will bring for me.
Foraging for love was all about being left
empty hearted in the return of loyalty.

~Shweta Gautam
@_loveforwords_

Foraging for love was my heart starving.
I was a weed, begging for a gardener.

~Heini Talip
@missfinnpoet

Foraging for love was always a journey of hearts to find a ray of sunshine during the dark, just like finding a hope in a world full of hopelessness. It's not about finding love, it's about finding one's soul to live through the darkness

~Aafreen Ahmed
@i.soulfulgirl

Foraging for love left me empty and dry,
My heart a desert of cobwebbed yearnings.
See ,the more I foraged for love in you, the more I fell in love with you,
The less I loved myself.
Now I am an empty shell of the dreamer I used to be.

~Julie Stevenson
@j.s.poet

Foraging for love was a wild adventure she embarked on
to feed her soul,
and what an escapade for her heart did that unfold !

~Vanashree Yadav Gautam
@vignettes_by_v

Short Stories and Proses

LACERNATION

The memories I left behind of you my love under that deep shady tree are dying after a long wait. I am back, don't die, here are few drops of water I can offer. Wait for me let's die together then. I am a melancholic now characterized by bloom, let's again untwine the twings of grassy memories from our mystical past healing the hearty and mildly laceration with embrocating while it leaks the fragrances from the past.

~Ajay Sawant (@rumiet.ry)

YOUR DISAPPEARANCE MAKES HOUDINI CRY

He said,
"I know nothing of magic, or a simple card trick for that matter.
I live like casper; socially a back bencher.
And I've seen on televisions some of the greatest magicians,
but the way you vanished is such an ignition.
You see, I spent half my best years assessing how you did it,
constantly fighting to keep looking for you.
And this is all really funny cause' for a while there I went crazy.
And so in words of the great Houdini; 'I'm tired of fighting',
this is me giving in, you can take home your win".

~Bk Murumi (@bkmurumi)

HEARTS AND PROMISES ARE MEANT TO BE BROKEN

I blame you no more for what happened, because hearts and promises are meant to be broken. And while you never really did anything to make it better, you were only following the trends of the society. Like everyone else, the naked truths of life hit me late, that life isn't a fairytale, that I'm no romantic character of a novel who get their happy endings. Happy endings are fictional, the reality is cruel and harsh. Sometimes, even difficult to accept. Therefore I don't blame you for anything hereon. Everything was just another lesson to be more cautious about the choices I make in the future. It was just another round of my life. I let you go today and I wish you all the happiness of life. May you always be happy. And even if I'm no longer the reason you smile, I pray it never fades and it's probably the last time I'll say it, but this heart of mine will always have the same love for you no matter if we hold on or let go of each other.

~Shweta Gautam (@_loveforwords_)

VIBRANCY

There, from across the room. She's pouring sunshine into the hands of strangers and they'll watch, a field of sunflowers following their star. Her words plant little gardens upon the slope of my mind, and the flowerets will bloom as I tumble freely for those gentle eyes. She repaints the world in every hue, and never again will mine be simply colorless.

~Cassandra Wood (@cm.writer)

MEMORIES

Every night your memories peek from my eyes and roll down on my cheeks, making me smile but confused, Is it of the moments that I have spent with you or is it your absence that I feel with every breath.

~Gaurav Dubey (@the_unwanted_heart_feelings)

ANONYMOUS

Yes, you heard it right!
She wants herself to be anonymous for all that she writes..
Do you want to know why?
No!! It's not because she is ashamed of her words, she can never be.
for how can a person be contrite to something which helped her to get through all that you've put onto her. From the time you left her like a crumbled piece of paper making her believe she is nothing more than a worthless body living like a corpse, those were the words that gave her the strength, the courage to bring back her lost soul escaping from the world of darkness, holding on for light and letting herself pour her heart out in the best way possible releasing from the guilt and remorse of loving someone like you with utmost purity.

Yes, she wants herself to be anonymous for she doesn't want her story to be told in a manner which will hold you responsible for all what has happened to her. No matter what she says, only her heart knows she still can't get you out of her mind, her heart and probably from her soul too.
May be she doesn't want to let you go,
May be that's what love does to her ..

But what's the point of pondering over these things when you left her long back? Do you still bother to care a bit after all this time?

~Niksha Nath (@niksha_justanamateur)

SPEAK

Those promises which were left outspoken and those words that were broken still lie beneath the winks of my watery eyes poking it with disgust. Cause I loved everything but nothing returned.

~Ajay Sawant (@rumiet.ry)

SUPPORTED

She said "I need support while walking. Life would become difficult for you"
"That gives me one more opportunity to hold your hand forever" he replied putting a ring in her finger.

~Dhanlaxmi Kumaresan
(@penning_down_my_thoughts)

LOVE CAN BRING SUFFERINGS

After many years they bumped into each other...
"Mom who was he?"
"He was the one who taught your mother that love can bring suffering too"

~Nischita Nibedita (@nischitanivedita)

NATURE MORALS

Dear nature your generosity always made me feel you
are my biggest eternal love.
Every nature's season implies to emotions of a human
and implicitly nature portrays image of a human
behavior, it always treats you as a family member until
your journey on this planet ends

~Chitrapu Ravali (@ravalisonu)

ART OF PRETENSION

Jiya liked it when people would call her cold or mean, probably because that was the only thing she couldn't be. She always had a thing for old, ruined and dilapidated things, so it was no surprise when they once found her sleeping in the graveyard at four in the morning, dressed in her favorite yellow colored skirt.

Jiya and I got to know each other through a social media platform where she had written in a post "to pretend well is an art", and soon I was confessing that I'm really terrible at pretending, and that sometimes, it's suffocating trying to conceal my feelings all the time.

I guess my confession made Jiya happy as it gave her a sense of superiority, given the odds of her impeccable familiarity with pretence.

Last week I received a package from Jiya with a letter attached to it, and it had just a line with a smile emoticon, written, "I am leaving for Arctic." I opened the package and it shone bright like the sun, it was favorite yellow colored skirt. And as I feared, this was the last time I ever heard from her.

You know Jiya, it's really sad but the emoticon was a message enough that you're never coming back. And now that I think of it Jiya, you were right. To pretend well is indeed just an art, and perhaps I am getting better at it with time. In fact, you know what- I don't miss you. Yes, I don't miss you at all.

~Arpit Jain (@your_alter_ego)

BUILDING ME

For once I'd like it if a guy built me up like one of those exceptional temples. Spending the back breaking effort and time. Putting in the labour and love, creating something beautiful out of my sturdy yet breakable marble walls. Intricately placing my fragile glass windows throughout the centre of it all. Allowing the light to shine through me, illuminating my soul. Making even the angels above shed a tear of jealousy.

~Ashleigh Rayl (@ashrayl)

WE WOULD BE PERFECT

After years, I see you and I feel young.
My bones weightless and my eyelids little less heavy.
I find myself a dimension away from falling again.
My throat feels dry and I'm running out of words.
I wish to stay but I'd like to leave.
Stay because I want to and leave because I may not be
able to
take it anymore. I recall "We are a perfect metaphors for
the endless sky and the bottomless sea, we will look
great if we get together but that is never happening"

~Mrinalini Sarkar (@imrinalini)

RAIN AND ROOM

No it's raining outside ! I am wet within , under water of bath shower. Love feels like loneliness, with none it feels even more. I am getting wet inside my soul. This gloom and dripping of showers outside with no spark of light and I am suiting myself in draining my leaks. Torrential flow of emotions is down the sink while the shower flooding bathroom with me sitting wet in corner. In this little room I am suffocating with freshness of breath of the fragrance of first summer rain. My heart is vacant and 'll be aching for someone hypothetical.

~Ajay Sawant (@rumiet.ry)

FOREVER DEAL

In that moment of fading life at age of 72 he took her
hand crying & said don't you go .
I dare you
Because only I have the right to take Your breath away.

~Niyanta Sailor (@s.niyanta)

PERFECT LOVE

I won't say that loving you was difficult. It definitely wasn't. It just took me "few" nights to convince my inner self that it was just your anger, not you. You didn't want to abuse me; it was just a passing moment, a fleeting second where your anger outweighed your love. Those marks on my wrists, no they too weren't an issue for me. I reminded myself that when you love a person, you need to accept his phases and that was just a phase, a phase where your ego outweighed your love. The old jeans and my old friends still call me sometimes but I have shut the doors now. Salwar suits me and Facebook is a mere modernization of other dating apps, I heard you saying once. The makeup I got last year for rakhi was used as a gift for our older niece. You were right both the times, she loved it and I didn't need makeup as I have a man now in my life. Loving you wasn't much difficult, I just needed to change a part (whole) of me but that's okay. After all, it always was my responsibility to keep you happy

~ Sheetal Bhatta (@letters_inc)

Poetry

ROSE

I am a rose drying in someone's diary
just to know how much pain can wither me.

~ Gopika Menon (@your.poetrygirl_)

DIFFERENCES

My dust,
Your amber,

My summer,
Your December,

My spring,
Your fall ,

I bloom,
You dissolve.

~Shivanshi Pandey (@whiskpoetry)

FEATHERS

Nobody knows how she felt,
that day,
The white feathered bird
travelling from the north
with her wings soaring high,
until they cut down her feathers,
with their sword of inhumanity
in silence, she cried out
hoping they might listen to
the sound of her tears falling
but alas! poor bird,
she did not know,
the place she was travelling,
no longer belonged to her,
not even the wind,
that once played with her,
and carried her like a child .

~ Dhiman Saha (@poetryofdhiman)

I ‘LL ALWAYS LOVE

I will always love the glimmer in your eyes,
Even if it flickers for her.

~Kavya Rajendran (@kavyaraja98)

COLOURS OF LOVE

Amidst all those blacks and whites I used to see,
Your love made me realize there exist some greys too,
A grey which may or may not give answers being crystal clear,
but will tend to hold your breath till the time you learn to seek them in those blues too.
Yes, while waiting for our love to bloom I realized there exist some greys too!

~Niksha Nath (@niksha_justanamateur)

YOUR LOVE WON'T FADE

Drained the blood from my heart,
Washed my soul a million times,
Yet, your love failed to fade,
While I kept playing with those words said.

~Kavya Rajendran (@kavyaraja98)

WALL

Walls,
I've built them,
And bolstered
My own.

I've climbed them,
I've fashioned
A home.

They've sheltered,
I've hid,
Forgotten to
Live.

Walls,
Forgive me,
I'm letting
Love in.

~Jayme Smith (@jlsmith_odist)

"19'TEEN"

I lost my tin around July,
In it, I had saved nineteen teens
Hoping to deliver it at your doorstep as souvenir of our love
Having broken your nineteenth tin, in search for a key out of these tinned teens

So I wrote this letter nineteen times,
Because I want to be your final Knight,
Knitting your nineteen flaws into a nineteenth star,
See I've sketched your smile ninety nine times,
But today, I perfected your charm
My candle flame fell to a slumber harmonizing with the flail touch of caramel absorbed by your eyes
And as if in acknowledgement, a speck of sunrise grazed my bedroom window

Then flickered our memories, teasing my closet bravery,
Remembering how you make the sunset envious when you blush,
How you sing the stars to a turmoil when you roll your glittering eyes,
How you render these little mice lifeless with your catwalk,
And how you set the breeze a listen when you laugh and play about

But on nights the nineteen star shoots a flare,
I'll write you the nineteen love letter
Because I've loved you in nineteen ways, and the nine say, you love me too.

~George Gumikiriza (@sir_wootridge.writes)

HIS INNER EMOTIONS

He said that he didn't care,
But the truth contrasted it all,
How life struck him was not fair,
He waited his entire life just for her one phone call,
Although he knew it won't ring.

~Aryan Lohia (@aryan._.lohia23)

OLD PAGES

Traces of you on me
smells so fresh,
when I read that old page
you fell in love with.
You said
those few words
living over there
always gives you
warmth of us.

Today in your absence
I looked at it
and I found love
as same as the one
which I saw in your eyes.
When you told me to stop
for our moment and a cup of coffee
in that coffee shop!

~Arati Khanal (@house_of_prose_and_poetry)

THAT DARKEST NIGHT

It is one of those baleful nights.
When shadows overpower lights.
When the sky is dark and starless,
As dark as my soul's darkness.
On nights like this I am awake,
The evil plans i make
To hurt, cripple and mutilate
And finish off those I hate.
On nights like this I think,
How to make their boats sink?
To kill at once or injure first?
How to quench my contempt's thirst?
I wish I could poison them slowly
And make them beg for my mercy,
But I will make sure there comes a day,
When all of them will fade
away,
Their defeats shall be their pyre,
Engulfed by the flames of my hatred's fire!

~Pritha Bose (@_the_colonel)

MY LOVE FOR YOU

My love for you
is a sunrise
showering on light
when you fight
with dusty storm...
It is a hope
hiding in your
small home
waiting for you
to come
and pick it up;
paint yourself
forget the sorrow
and fall in love
with every little thing
around you !

~Arati Khanal (@house_of_prose_and_poetry)

TOGETHER WE CAN

We go through ups and downs, but still nothing can tear us apart.
I know you as a friend, and I will always care,
Love, respect, and trust are the things we share
I know you as a person, I especially know you as a friend,
Our friendship is something that will never end
Right now, this second, this minute, this day,
Our friendship is here, is here to stay.
My friendship with you is special and true,
When we are together, we stick like glue.
When I'm in the darkness that need some light
When you're by my side, I know things are all right
Our friendship is so strong, it breaks down bars,
Our friendship is also bright, like the sun and the stars.
If we were in a competition for friendships, we would get gold,
Because responsibility and cleverness are the keys we hold.
I met you as a stranger, took you as a friend,
I hope our long friendship will never end.
Because no matter where we are, our friendship will last forever.

~Deepesh Katariya (@the_irksome_admirer)

SAVING MY LOVE

The sum of our love
could have filled oceans.
Yet, I want us to preserve it
in our hearts itself.
For what if others toxicate it
as they did to the oceans?

~Fahima Nizar (@fahima_nizar)

TIME

The truth is I always think about you
You are always on my mind
Time takes you further and further
away from me
I try to freeze time and I fail
But it's fine because time
Cannot take you out of my mind
In my mind , our time is limitless.

~Norah Arriya (@ruminatingsoul)

LOOKS

I wonder why people fall for looks,
I found most of the love and whole of my life in these books

~Astha Vyas (@vyas_astha)

PROMISES OF A BROKEN FOREVER

I want you to promise me you'll hold my hand...no not forever, but till the time your hands want to tighten every loosen grip between us!

I want you to promise me you'll walk by my side...no not forever, but till the time your feet doesn't want to part ways with mine!

I want you to promise me you'll love me...no not forever, but till the time your heart tells you I am the one who holds that special place in it!

Yes i want some promises from you of us being together but not forever that should last lifetime but till the time that forever counts a meaning to you.

For i don't want our love to end by a broken forever!
As they say "nothing lasts forever" but I want our forever to last till the time we want it to...

~Niksha Nath (@niksha_justanamateur)

ASH

Ashes ashes,
You don't fall down,
Sparks and embers fly,
From the moment you light me on fire.
Ashes ashes,
You didn't fall down,
When you dumped a bucket,
Of ice cold water on my heart,
Ashes ashes,
I did fall down.

~Brin Battisti (@_mybeautifulchaos___)

IN OTHER LIFE

In another world, in another life
If love wishes to touch me I would ask not to.
Because now I am tired.
A little broken.
A lot shattered.
I can no more bend to make it stay.
Because my back is broken by now I can't let it go.
Because everytime it does, it takes a part of me leaving
me incomplete.
In another world, in another life
I wish to be poetry to someone.
A poetry that will please him everytime he read.
A poetry that will chase him wherever he headed.
I won't have to smile back when he smile at me.
And not pretend to be something that I can never be.
In another world, in another life
I want to own the sky and live a dream.

~Mrinalini Sarkar (@imrinalini)

DEEPER

And with every sip
I take
I fall further and further
Into my imagination
And we are so happy there
We are intertwined there
But sadly our love
Only exists
In the final drops
Of my empty bottle
And as hard as I have tried
My cup never seems
To be filled
I just can't journey back
To reality
I can't journey back
To the place where
You don't love me
So
Bottoms up

~Cheyenne Tyler Jacobs (@shewillspeak)

MIDNIGHT LANDSCAPE

On the dimmed landscape of midnight,
The frost between the oak trees,
seems to have lighten up the moonlight.
And something brighter has awakened,
in the chamber of the dreary woods,
near the half-frozen lake.
The pretty night has become radiant,
Hence it complements the coldness,
that has already silenced the vast land,
and spread its wings beyond the cloudy mountains.

~ Dhiman Saha (@poetryofdhiman)

MY DREAM

I'm still dreaming of our love
not being a product of my own imagination.

~ Allegra Minerva (@a.m.doespoems)

BRICKS

And with every word I am laying bricks around you,
That I firm with the concrete of my actions.
To trap you in the dungeons of my soul,
And never set free again.

~Ajay Sawant (@rumiet.ry)

HEALS

Your smile travels through my heart,
And heals my wounds and scars at a glance

~Shruti Agrawal (@writershruti)

HIS LOVE, NOT FOR ME

Your love for her,
Don't you lord it over me!

~Allegra Minerva (@a.m.doespoems)

TORMENTED HEART

I hate
how I begged
for you you stay
not once
not twice
but every single time
you got up to leave

I hate
how you relished
the exquisite taste
of my tears
of my fear
and came back
for another series

And I hate
how I relied
on your very being
to feel complete
to feel 'me'
feeling your withdrawal
like a smoker's from nicotine

So I hate how
when I found
the courage
to let you go
you walked out on me
took the keys
and locked
the door

~Khadija Inam (@k.inam_)

LETTERS OF MY LOVE

I've loved you like,
I've loved my Poetries,
Pouring my heart out,
And letting my emotions flow,
To the unknown lands,
That you show.

~Shruti Agrawal (@writershruti)

THE FALL

Please, let me see you,
I'm just trying to love you.

Show you I'll be here even when
You shut yourself in that barbed-wire fence,
And act like I don't know you;
like I'm worse than sin, but sometimes you forget,
let your defenses slip
lose your grip,
let yourself feel content
ride the high,

Then like a light switch, flip your shit,
no warning sign, but i'm ready this time.

I'm pushed back up against the ledge,
tensed and numb, awaiting descent,

This is what we have become,
heaven-sent?

Still burns like hell, but maybe I've become an arsonist,

'cause I don't mind the sting, as long as I see a flicker of
you.

I can't resist,
now falling free,
hoping it's the sea and not the concrete.

~Kyla Newman (@thewritingloft)

A RELATION AGO

A relationship ago,
I was a different person.

~Edwin John A (@e.j.tulik)

CAN I BE THE REASON?

Can I be the reason
of your happiness ?
Can I be the one
to wipe your tears ?
Can I have all your deepest scars ?
And can I be the other half of your heart ?

~Shruti Agrawal (@writershruti)

OUR EXISTENCE

He is everything, I am nothing at all,
But he never left me on my own,
He has a massive throne on the sky,
But he resides in every drop of my blood,
He is my creator, who gave me a soul,
And blessed me thousand times more,
Beauty he created, makes me sure,
He's breathtaking of them all,
He is merciful who forgives me,
And never stops loving me no matter what,
He pour his essence in my soul,
And bloom with it fragrance of love,
When he wrote 'he loves me' ,
I believed him, it means for eternity.

~AK Stars Above (@whispersofbrokenheart)

MY MISTAKE

Whilst,
I let you in totally for me ,
I realized my err,
My heart broken to scads,
There was nothing I could do,
Rather have a long wait,
With gathering pieces of my love.
To be in someone's accrue.
Wanting for some ardent love,
Healing me with morning dew
With sowing the seeds of love in the warmth of my cardiac bed.
Fertilizing it with the decaying memories hard dead .

~Ajay Sawant (@rumiet.ry)

FRAGMENTS

What if we ever bear the fragments of
Rising
Healing
Hoping
And
Flowering
From the genes we inherit
Wouldn't the world have been a better place?

~Ajay Sawant (@rumiet.ry)

UNWANTED LOVE

Bleeding heart and weeping eyes;
I watch you be with the girl you desire.
Both of you undeniably shine,
unlike me who cannot confide,
These feelings --
these unwanted feelings of mine,
Tell me, how much pain do I need to hide ?
How many times do I need to smile,
even though I am not the one by your side?

~Agnes Belen Operiano (@dec_embre)

THE DIFFERENCE

Yes--
At times, I'm naive
I choose to see good
In everyone
Because there is

Even after I'm hurt,
Which happens rather easily,
But everyone deserves love

And what if they've never
Known it?
What if they've confused it
For pain?

Maybe that's why I'm here--
To show you the difference.

~Jayme Smith (@jlsmith_odist)

BROKEN BUTTERFLY

You left me alone without saying goodbye,
shattered, broken and crushed to cry....

May be you thought I'll be another "damsel in distress"
or a "broken butterfly",
Sorry dear, for now you will see how I fly high!!!

~Niksha Nath (@niksha_justanamateur)

MELANCHOLY

Fierce storm on my mind,
destroying the garden in my heart,
Melancholy penetrating all my veins;
in my body after our separation.
I would give anything to see you,
just to cease the storm.

~Oderuth Oozeer Mehneez (@dreamy.words)

WHEN I THINK OF YOU

Whenever I think of you,
my tongue dances behind my lips.
My hips ache for those,
rough callused hands grasping,
My chestnut hair begs to be pulled.
This flame of passion ignites,
running through my whole being,
burning me alive.
And the only thing,
that could put me out is you.

~Ashleigh Rayl (@ashrayl)

THE FIRST

I could feel him on me,
His weight pushed away
the weight of my insecurities,
I looked into his eyes which were blazing,
the fire we were burning was seeping through.
His hands grazed my back
leaving his traces all over.
His lips over mine sucking
the air between us.
We were breathing as one,
Our hearts beating as one,
Our bodies struggling to merge,
The air between us shied away
And we were finally united.

~Gursimar Kaur (@pen_fight)

TELL ME MORE

Tell me about magic,
The loneliness that rhymes your heart.
Your vacant side,
And the chest wanting a warm hug.

Your heart ache is nothing but of isolation,
The scars are sparsity of the arid barren lands of savannah.
This heart with vacant fertility,
Is not just jovial and kind, its divine and sacrine,
Every more than anyone you deserve.

As every glimpse of you gets me cognizance of me being less deserving of that bedazzled bewitching soul which you hold.

~Ajay Sawant (@rumiet.ry)

STARS IN THE SKY

I love you,
Like stars love the sky.
They're there during the day,
Silently stay,
Hide behind the light,
They're there during the nights,
Shining brightly,
Scaring away the dark.

~Gursimar Kaur (@pen_fight)

MY HALLUCINATIONS

Those hands of yours caressing
my hair,
making me feel there's nothing in this world
that could take this feeling away from me,
nothing that could ever lessen your love for me....

Those intertwined fingers of ours,
filling the spaces between our hearts
planting the seeds of a never ending love,
beginning of a story that could last forever....

That moment when your eyes met mine,
calming the storm blooming since ages
however giving rise to a new fire that could burn
everything down to ashes...

Those moments spent with you,
offering me the sense of togetherness
letting me dream of a perfect tomorrow,
giving rise to new hopes and desires leaving no space for
sorrows...

For a moment i thought,
everything could be perfect like a fairytale,
everything could last forever....

For in that moment may be
my hallucinations overpowered me
Cause I forgot love is an illusion and
expecting happily ever after in this brutal world is
nothing less than heading towards darkness without
knowing a way to come back!!

~Niksha Nath (@niksha_justanamateur)

ROSES FROM MY GARDEN

A garden full of roses so red
I was the gardener,
like a mother to them.
You passed by to watch me take care,
And our eyes met,
The roses now had a mother and a father as well,
I was gone for a while, trusting you with my roses who were my life.
You plucked them out and painted them white.
And when I got to know, you never loved
I cried and cried for you had taken my life.
And my roses once red were never the same again.

~Ayema Faisal (@poetesstic)

DAY OF OUR FRIENDSHIP

The day you became my friend,
all my problems came to an end.
The glow of your personality,
energizes my soul till eternity.
Whenever you are sad and hurt,
I swim in the bottomless tank of guilt,
the wounds don't heal,
for they are more than I can deal...
Everytime I look at you,
I feel there's something new.
My friend, my dearest friend,
I don't know what makes you
so special in my heart,
It's been a longtime
that we are together,
the happiness and sorrow
that we share with each other.
I just love you and
will continue to do so
as it's my heart's desire
to never let you go....

~Anoop Kumar Sureka (@_i_m_anoop_)

DONT

Don't lie,
At least not to yourself,
And please don't even try to convince.

~Ajay Sawant (@rumiet.ry)

FREEDOM

Seeking answers,
Heart wants what it wants.
The war inside her heart was over,
She had set him free forever;
Her soul cried out its tears,
Soon she reached out for her fears;
"Sun never leave the earth" he'd told,
Irony laughed as she stood there cold;
Hoping he would have ever heard
What her heart said,
How slowly she was being slayed;
She fell on her knees, left shattered,
And panted for her breath,
For all she searched now was death;
Slowly each breath she took,
Engulfing her inside too deep,
She wished the memories had a leap;
He never knew what was behind that beautiful smile,
As she walked away from him
miles and miles...

~Shreyashi Deb (@__bubble_boo__)

THEN IT TURNED NIGHTMARE

Unspoken Answers,
When did she fall in love so deep?
He touched the core of her heart as his words embraced her in a bond of care.
Why were his eyes so magnetic?
Those smoothness and intense depth of his eyes; she couldn't resist rather than to stare.
Why couldn't she stop thinking of him?
He filled her thoughts with sparkles in her dreams that were so rare.
Why was her heart so stubborn?
Her heart fought so hard as her feelings for him was ware.
Why didn't her heart give up?
His love hurted, and she knew that pain was made to bare.
Why was it hard to accept the truth?
The heart wants what it wants; it won't have had a share.
What was his existence in her?
Deadly nights had turned into soulful breezes; without his thoughts it was her darkest nightmare.

~Shreyashi Deb (@__bubble_boo__)

IN THE NAME OF LOVE

In the name of love,

Keep staring at my naked eyes,
Adore the beauty of my face without facial,
Get yourself lost in my messy hair,
Find me in shape with my unshaped body,
Tell me I look gorgeous with those outgrown eyebrows,
See me sparkling without any ornaments,
That's all I want in the name of love.

~Khushbu Patel (@_khushi_writes)

THE PINK WALL

Pretty skirts,
Doll house,
Pink room,
Elegant blouse,
All her life she has been bound,
To the norms of being a girl very sound,
She grew up,
Now she wore,
Short dresses,
That showed so much more,
Thongs,
Panty hose and,
all that stuff
She never understood,
And she couldn't bluff,
For she was a lady and she had to do,
Whatever it takes for a man to woo.
Her mother insisted to cross the lines,
As she never had a boyfriend,
She could call mine,
In her thirties,
A virgin,
She was,
A tormenting truth,
A tormenting past,
Why was she like that she asked herself so many times,
Her mother shushed her up,
Holding a crime,
One day in blues,
She found someone,
For once in her life she wasn't on a run,
She felt safe she felt sound,
As if the world started to make sense,
For she has been found,

The love of her life made her happy and free,
For he wasn't a He but a She,
Yes she was a girl,
But not a lady after all,
She was a queer,
And has finally jumped the wall,
Her family disowned her,
But she was okay,
For love conquers all,
Whether it's straight or gay.

~Khushbu Patel (@_khushi_writes)

CITY STREETS

Running among the trains,
Passing by the buses,
holding my work bag,
And dodging all the fusses.
The world called out ,
With its big tower and city lights,
I love being a part of these noisy nights.
Where people don't sleep and peace not to be found,
Yet they find happiness in all those loud sounds.
I love seeing the crowds outside the coffee shop,
It's 7 in the morning and people are bursting out,
It may be odd or it may be not,
the city streets catch my breath
no matter what.
The cold hard pavement i walk all day long,
The strangers I pass by think about their own songs.
Nature and hills are not beyond my contemplation,
But don't you think they are only meant for vacation?
I mean see this right here where we live,
This street, this place, this whole city is exclusive...
The rushing of people,
The speeding of vehicle,
The adrenaline rush,
Oh damn I love this so much.

~Preeta Roy (@in.the.autumn.of.words)

HE KNEW AND HE HOLDED

I was quiet and he understood,
I was falling apart and he held my hand.
I was tired and he gave me hope,
He didn't give up on me,
I was short tempered and he was my nerve cooler.
He didn't give up on me.
I screamed in anger but he kept calm,
I said leave me alone but he never left my side.
I lost the way; he became my guide.
He didn't give up on me,
He gave me infinity.

~Myra Dutta (@fairies_and_lust)

JUST A MEMORY

It's been a year now, since we stopped being we,
I bet you have forgotten all about me.
I remember the early days of our love story,
When our love blossomed like the cherry trees in spring,
Our hearts used to beat together, and soared in the air
like a bird
with wings.

Then came summer, passion and heat reigning over us...
We let our desires consume our souls, and burn us down
to ashes of love.

Fall arrived, my heart full of hope,
And I waited for the pieces to fall into place like the
leaves,
But instead, I was left to cope with the aftermath of
drifting away from you,
Just like the autumn leaves do.

Winter heralded cold, dreary days,
"They will never make it through," I heard them say,
I wanted to prove them wrong,
But, I guess our love wasn't strong.
I just want you to know that, even though we didn't
work,
I still miss my cute little dork.

~Deblina Bhattacharya (@author_deblina)

FLAVOURS OF LOVE

As I fell In love,
The beams of blazing sun shoot out,
like gold strings against my pale sky.
As you touched me, I
Couldn't help but melt Into you,
like the Sun kisses the Sea and lose itself in it.
As we fall apart, my
Heart broke into two,
like a green leaf burst into scarlet and rust.
As I missed you, all
The barren trees rhymed my insides,
like a stiff frozen layer cover the place.
As our eyes met again,
All the hard feelings melted,
like symphonies of colors splash into the snowy park.

~ AK Stars Above (@whispersofbrokenheart)

BLACK BILE

My Black Bile turned into sangfroid,
My Consciousness sunk into that numb well,
My head began to "spin", in the mesmerizing virgin art of her's,
All I want tonight is to let your sweet pecks devour me to the fullest,
And to let your fingertips untie all my senses,
All I want is to silhouette the eastern sky in the shades of golden with our kisses,
Such that for eons my lips could tell your story,
In all possible tenses.
And all I want is just to celebrate our sign of love with the gleamed treetops emerging owing to sunrays..

~Harshal Bajaj (@harshalbajaj06)

FAR YET SO CLOSE

We were far,
Yet so close,
For the sky bought us closer,
It connected us with a kiss in infinity...

~Saumya Singh (@saumyeah)

TRUE COLOURS

Blinded by your love,
Against my parents,
With you, I eloped,
When you showed me your true colours,
Thereafter - I realized,
Your love itself was a slippery slope,
In a fewer moments-
And just fewer words,
All the love from him,
Is all I want to collect, Alas!
It was too late-
When I realized that,
I was building my love,
On the grave of my self-respect,
I was a beautiful book,
That was crumpled,
And burnt to ashes,
Even before It was read.

~Harshal Bajaj (@harshalbajaj06)

SAD TRUTH OF LOVE

In the world where loyalty and pure soul is so rare,
some creepy eyes search for body so fair.
In the world where you want to be loved for being sweet and clever,
Isn't that strange?
you're surely loved bug for your navel.
In the world where everyone says: "someone craving for your purity is hard to find",
don't you think?
It's easier to find someone craving for your body.
With changing generations the essence of love has changed,
Love has become a loser for now lust always wins over.

~Jahnvi Raol (@untold._.feels)

CLOSED BOOK

I had closed the book which held the seeds of our memories
Planted in the middle of pale pages
And framed inside for ages.
They won't live, they'd die,
I believed.

But, today my eyes accidentally fell
On the drawer which had many secrets to tell.
From years it was untouched
So I could see it covered with dust.

Remnants of past crawled slowly
Onto my palm
And then spread over me
It was the knob which I could see
A twist and turn, then a pull toward me
I found flowers blooming in the book
I had closed
Which held seeds of our memories

~Disha Dahiya (@disha.writes)

CITYLIGHTS

Those city lights sparkling so bright,
Those metro fights impossible to respite,
Those never ending drives along with flickering of lights,
Everything so nice except the girl sitting aside,
Hard to guess whether she was lost in her world or her world was lost somewhere.
So many questions were there,
Whose answers were still to be find nowhere,
Maybe those city lights doesn't really fascinate her,
Maybe nothing was there to engage her,
Maybe... Maybe she just wanted to know,
Was she really meant to be there
Or
Was it just the destiny playing it's game with her?

~Niksha Nath (@niksha_justanamateur)

I BELONG HERE

I belong here beside you
With your palm embracing mine, and my toes playing
with yours till nine,
I promise this playful love won't end, but I don't believe
in infinities, it's not true and never meant to bend
I'm dribbling myself with oneirataxia,
Infinity is a fantasy and you are my reality
I do have faith in 'forever and always'
Which makes us merge our ways.

~Disha Dahiya (@disha.writes)

TOGETHER

We saw the sun rise together & now only ,
I shall watch it set..

~Saumya Singh (@saumyeah)

CHANCE

Give me a chance,
To wake up by your side,
Every day,
To kiss your cheek every morning.

Give me a chance,
To make your morning a little more brighter,
And your night a little less dark,
Cause if you do.

Then I'll give you a chance too,
A chance to get pampered by me every other day,
A chance to never feel lost ever,
Cause I promise to be by your side forever.

Let's give each other a chance,
To love and be better,
A chance,
To grow old together.

~Riya Nagpal (@serene_purpose)

TILL ETERNITY

It started with just one hello,
Now I can't let you go,
The face of an angel that I see in you,
Has become an addiction I didn't knew

Always in my thoughts,
Tearing through my dreams,
A life without you,
would be a shattered dream,

These butterflies,
Shy smiles,
The way you move,
hips don't lie,

I don't know how to say it,
To make it sound so true,
If my dreams turn into reality,
I want my love to last till eternity

~ Aakash Kumar Nanda (@aakash_kumar_5)

TILL ITS MY NAME

So long the way, I began my steps,
Don't know how far I am,
Could I be there in the oath of faith?
Stepping my feet where destiny came,
I solemnly found solace beneath your shine of hopeful flame.
And I am here in search of me,
My destiny rolled under stranded aim,
Oh! I wish you to hold me up,
And keep coddling till it is my name.

~ Akeel Bhat (@akeelbhat)

LETS CHOOSE

Let's choose our own sky,
Let's choose our own moon,
Lets choose our own lie
Lets choose not to swoon.

Let's sit in the corner of the room,
Let our memories dance in the middle,
Let not our pain exhume,
Let not our love become a riddle.

Let me be your option and her your choice,
Cause this time I don't want to be the game
I don't want to be the one you blame,
I wish to be the memory you rejoice,
Not the well of tears in your voice.

~ Payal Hora (the_comely_ingenue)

HIS LOVE WAS DULL

The sky turned pink,
Like her love for you.
Seeping through,
The sadness of the blue.

But how was she to know,
That love in his heart was black.
It absorbed all her hues,
To reflect nothing back.

~Aboli Mane (@writer_abby)

CYNIDE

Next time when you kiss me,
You will taste cyanide on my lips.
Because, I want you to die a peaceful death,
And not like me, who kissed the blade on your lips and
bled to death every day!

~ Payal Hora (the_comely_ingenue)

ENVELOPES OF LOVE

Between the sleeves of the envelope,
Their love ran sugar sweet.
Ornate as an elegant font,
Yet aged like an old book leaf.

When the ink dripped indigo,
Their mind flowed with the script.
When the nib scratched the paper,
Their hearts clenched as though ripped.

Their verses remained etched,
Hers in an unruly squiggly trail.
His in an exquisite flowing scrawl,
Love flourished through snail mail.

~Aboli Mane (@writer_abby)

WILDERNESS

I let her go,
As she belonged to the wild,
I was the last sojourn,
In her journey,
I remember how her bones,
Started to crumble,
Yet her heart,
Desired for the destination,
She was dying so I gifted her,
Some breathes of mine,
After all I have always loved those,
Who never give up,
For I know how it feels,
When you can't reach home.

~Prashant Pundir (@aliterarysoul)

WILD EMBERS

Once he loved a girl,
Grey as a Winter's fog.
So he tinted her cheeks,
With blossoms gathered in Spring.

And streaked her eyes with kohl,
From enchanting Autumn nights.
Set fireflies in her dark hair,
Glowing like Summers bright.

Gazing at her reflection,
She locked him in an embrace.
For the colours of his devotion,
Stuck fast despite the Rain.

~Aboli Mane (@writer_abby)

LET ME

Let me tune in with the divine rhythm,
let me put my heart out,
let me feel the vibes and
dance along here with you
in this beautiful night...

Let me pour my thoughts here,
let me dwell upon this ink,
let me live those moments again and
feel like you're still here with me
somewhere shining bright...

Let me smile through the pain,
let me fight back from tears,
let me just love you the way i used to and
believe that everything is still alright...

Let me hold on to your memories,
let me reminisce our beautiful past,
let me be with you till the end to
always have a place in your heart...

Let me...Just let me be myself again!!!

~Niksha Nath (@niksha_justanamateur)

HE'S A MASTERPIECE

His smile is an illusion.
His soul is magic.
His eyes are a pieces of art,
And his touch is gentle indelible.

~Ayushi Jain (@ayushi_sancheti)

MUG AND MY DAIRY

With taking away all my sorrows,
Nights relaxed me with peace,
I felt light when darkness fades my heaviness.
I love you,
Said the mug of my black coffee,
I love you more,
Giggled the pages of my favourite dairy,
They are my companions in secret keeping so I love them too.
My pain smiled through my dairy,
Lost or found,
Whether I am in Love or with lust,
They know me the best.

~Ishita srivastava (@ish_writings)

LONGING

I long to touch your lips even in dreams with open eyes,
That waist I wanted to touch with many tries,
Your hour glass body mesmerizes me,
I wonder when will you sit and speak love to me.

The first time I felt your skin,
I wanted to feel you more for a reason akin,
Ask you questions deep within your heart,
Touch your bosoms for a love cut.

Exploring your curves that I craved all nights,
But felt you just for a fortnight,
Will you come back to sit beside me,
For a life to be fulfilled by you and me.

~Ratnadeep Acharya (@writes._._deep)

I "LL LET YOU IN

Let me sleep,
Let me feel you beside me,
Making your way through my dreams, to my bed,
Such a thrust of warming touch,
Bunch of clutch,
A bit much
As much.
Touch my untouched heart,
Be my crutch when life sucks,
I will let you be my hutch,
And crush your love in my skin's crust.

~Ishita srivastava (@ish_writings)

OUR COSMOPOLITAN LOVE

Standing in the metro just beside you,
The fingers touching for reasons so new,
Walking down the Middleton street,
I wished I could kiss you for a treat.

The smell of old times walking down the tram line,
I dreamt to hold your hands for my soul to shine,
These monuments of history that we visited,
Did you feel my heart, the one that can be trusted.

The city lights showed emotions of passion,
I hoped for a chance to love you with compassion,
But you never let me come close you see,
We could have done magic for ages to see.

~Ratnadeep Acharya (@writes._._deep)

TOGETHER

My heart flutters when I see you smile.
It dances rhythmically with joy.
I want to be with you.
But my shyness gets the better of me.
I need to get away from you before my heart ruptures.
And when I am away, my heart yearns for you.
Yet I won't never let you know,
For we are not meant to be.

~Disha Mohanty (@__lost._.wanderer__)

CONFLICTS IN MY THOUGHTS

Sometimes I don't understand what makes me think
about you all the time
Your hatred
Or
My love.

~Shreya Gupta (@_creouscule__)

LUST

First a blessing than a curse,
Yes you loved me but just for lust.

~Shreya Gupta (@_creouscule__)

SADNESS CAN'T BE HELPED

Can't help myself from feeling sad,
The feelings I had from you are something I
never had.

Trying to move on and let all of it go,
Realizing time without you goes by slow.

It's hard not to ask the question why,
I still like you, there is no reason for me to lie.

Knowing something so good got away;
I am trying to figure out
if there is something I could say.

~Rohit Das (@guchupoofficial)

DISTANCES

They say home is where the heart is.
Mine was 1200 km away.

~Disha Mohanty (@__lost._.wanderer__)

MEMORIES LIE IN MY HEART

The distance is tearing us apart.
But I can hold the memories in heart.
I hate being this far.
I feel like I can't express the things I need to say.
Whether you like it or not I'll always be here,
to wipe away every single tear.
Sometimes I get so close but feel so far,
All I'm asking is please don't hurt.
I'm hurt where only I can see.
I wish I could tell the things I wanted to.
I wish you were here with me every day.
Though I know some things I did to you were cruel.

~Rohit Das (@guchupoofficial)

BEST

The best love is the kind that awakens the soul, that
makes us reach for more, that plants a fire in your heart
and bring peace to your mind.
That's what I hope to give you forever.

~Guru (@__it_wasnt_me____)

YOU ARE

You are my last bite,
That can't be shared.

You are my last page,
That has no space for any another.

You are my last rhythm,
That whole life satisfaction.

You are my last memory,
That keeps me alive,
You are my last love,
That can break me forever.

~Soniya S (@feelings_awestruck)

DON'T

Don't show him,
Don't tell him,
Don't let him know what you feel for him,
You can't bear the rejection.
Oh girl, you have so many imperfections.
Don't even try to do it,
Because you know there's no space for you in his heart to fit.
That's what the mind says when you've a crush,
And nothing just happens except the situation being harsh.
What are you afraid of?
To lose the precious friendship?
Go tell him, listen to your heart,
Just be conscious about what you do and say to him, "I LOVE YOU".

~Srishti (the_bleeding_pen._)

LOVE ISN'T A SPHERE

Your love is nothing but a lesson for me.
A lesson which changed my whole life.
I never imagined that love can be so evil and revengeful.
Our love was like,
Tea without sugar,
Sea without shells,
A church without bells,
Sky without stars.
Like a poet without pen and a desert without rain,
Maths without numbers and rain in November.
Like a winter without warmth but true in some form.
You don't love me, but I still have all those memories treasured,
created by "US"
which no one has the power to snatch from me

~Shamita Singh (@amyra_19)

VIRTUALITY

Apart,
For months on ends,
With no end in sight,
Hearts beats as one across the miles,
And grow stronger with distance and time.
Magnifying the moments of virtual joy,
Stolen from busy lives,
With each heartbeat leading closer to reunion,
Both hoping that it was real.

~Lesley Worthington (@worthywrites)

PROMISES

Some couple of years back,
We condensed into each other
Promising forever.
But this promise lays decaying today
When I see the love you talked of, fade away.
So today, I choose to walk back to my home which is no more mine.
I decide to walk alone this time.
But the smell of an old lover's skin pulls me back.
It rains and I feel the hands of your love trying to condense me in, yet again.
I see spring evenings turning winter nights
Convincing me to seek for what I had left behind.

~Mrinalini Sarkar (@imrinalini)

CLOUDS

Scary clouds often come with the most beautiful rains.

~Ami Johri (@26_amisba)

IS IT LOVE ?

Confused and scared,
I thought I knew love,
I thought I was in love,
I thought I married for love,
And then...,
You,
And now I ,
Must destroy lives,
In order to abide true love,
How can this be,
In Love?

~Lesley Worthington (@worthywrites)

TIMBRE

How many times have I laid here and wondered,
Why does your scent lingers remains within your absence.
Playing peek-a-boo with my nostrils;
My senses plunge deeply in the forever lands of your aroma
And I am caught within its fragrance.
I still quiver whenever our lips brush
And your eyes reflect, how much you love me.
Feeling their hunger for my passion,
It makes me smile to know that your love and care stays ignited inside just for me;
Perhaps it is written upon our face,
Well lit within our smiling eyes
And told within those strong curvatures at our lips that shouts joy,
We found melody in love's timbre.
Perhaps that is why I am always humming to this rhythm,
While feeling your presence and remembering,
What it means to be in love.

~Sahana Kumar (@sahana_kruti)

LIFE

Life is a beautiful song if you read the lyrics carefully.

~Ami Johri (@26_amisba)

SHINE

My love
See how your soul
builds a new empire
with those broken pieces
which went through darkness
and still stands tall
to shine.

~Aanchal Rout (@27.91del)

THEN

If I'm the darkness in the sky
in between those stars,
Then, you are my moon
which is admired by all
but owned by me.

~Fiza Farheen (@Its_her_thought)

IT HURTS BADLY

When a beautiful heart is broken,
Everything seems just dark all around,
Everything seems over,
There is no hope left,
When someone cheats...
From now on your life is like
Hatred,
Depressed,
Tears never stop,
When someone cheats,
It hurts badly.

~Khushboo Jain (@khush0133)

DOLLHOUSE LOVE

Love on chalks..
But she used his cheeks as board!
Love on dolls..
But she played with him!
Hide and seek, her favourite game..
Hidden for a while!
And now she typed in her style.

~Roopi (@wordsworld_life)

PRESENCE

Wordless days.
Wordless nights.
Only when he left I realized that presence mattered more than words.

~Rachitha M. R. (@17_rach)

YOU

Lift my feet from the ground,
Will you teach me to fly for every stound?
Cause angel you are of my life,
There's evanescence of my sorrow due to your smile.

Don't hold my hand, I'll just follow your shining hues,
Don't want stars I desire to sleep on moon, will you be my muse?
You can bring all my anxieties on a hold,
Covering me with your wings when it'll be cold.

~Liza Momin (@ecstasy_in_words)

HEART REWIND'S MEMORIES

I'm amazed,
how even in those busy hours of the day,
My heart takes a moment
to sit back and think about you.

~Fiza Farheen (@Its_her_thought)

FINAL TOUCH

Your red eyes don't scare me,
Your ferocious passion doesn't anxitude me,
The way your nails dig into the skin of my arms,
Even that formation of unique tattooed tsunamis don't hurt me,
So let it shade with my blood,
Let your teeth give it a final touch.

~Liza Momin (@ecstasy_in_words)

HAZE

The crow showed on elm, she knew letter would come,
And it did come.
Breathing heavily, she inhaled love from scribbled
hearts.
Then she married an old.
For the letters have disappeared, and the lover too.
In waiting lies no hope and return,
For the crow is dead, haze and snow.

~Aisha Shaikh (@aishashaikh121)

SPACE

You left me crying
Thinking I need space
But without you the space too
Leaves me crying

~Moiz Mahabaleshwarwala (@quilleddiaries)

TALK OF ME

Don't talk of moon; of roses
Talk of me instead.
For they are merely metaphors,
An essence that completes me.

~Aisha Shaikh (@aishashaikh121)

DIPPED IN ROYAL BLUE

Can we write a story together in all the shades of blue?
I'll build you this house and in it we'll keep all our secrets.
And a lovely little garden, but honey,
we'll have the bluest
tulips and we'll scourge the earth for the roses that glow the most.
And maybe, we can make this little family, ten kids and five puppies.
There's just this one thing. I want a room all to myself,
I may occasionally let you in, but an empty room styled with shelves on every wall,
And ironic as it seems, I'll fill it with us.
My love, it was in the fiery summer of May that I first laid my eyes on you,
That night, for the party that my father had planned in hopes that I'll be noticed,
I chose the least frilly dress and wore the brightest smile, politely.
And of course, a lady mustn't go bare necked, so a simple diamond pendant
My mother's dowry, hung proudly round my neck. And it did the trick.
I had caught the eye of the handsome man with a heavy beard, and a heavier wallet.
So much so he wrote me letter,
A gentlemanly remark of how my courtesy was just so feminine and graceful
And of how my sun hat stayed titled just right,
All dipped in royal blue.

~Anna Cherian (@sparklesandink)

YOU AND I

You and I,
Encapsulated in the air of our love,
Standing under the moonlit sky,
Stared at our undressed hearts,
Uniting to create a mystical soul,
Weaving ribbons of gold between our breathes,
Unable to escape the gravity of our love,
Surrendered before each other keeping our abyss inside.
Forgetting every worry that blossomed in our heads.
Meeting our tribe and discovering our calling,
Blown by the windfall of our warmth,
Yes darling, I still remember this is how we made love
that night.

~Niva Kalita (@feelings_voiced)

SINNED LOVE

As the moon and the Pleiades go down
And the tick of the clock fails to match the pace of our ruptured hearts,
Inarticulate cries from my drunken eyes flow
as you take me on my first trip of that wilderness that laid within me
With your fingers rolling down my sacred parts,
A flow of honey from my belly I could feel,
While the trembling-firm-smoothness of your silky soul rubbed against mine,
Exploring my sharp and unexpected edges, revealing in each of my curves,
Violently making love,
Pulling me backward into your forward thrusts
And calling my name in whispers as I moan into your ears,
I realize I can drink this sin for lifetime.

~ Somya Thakur (@sammiediaries)

IT 'LL ALWAYS BE YOU

Turns out some feelings
stayed back as prisoners.
I'm trying to fight it.
JIHAD.
And it's rather pathetic
cause' every time
the liquor lands my mouth,
I start to wonder about yours.

(please tell me you feel the same)

~Bk Murumi (@bkmurumi)

I AM NOT A MAT

I am sorry that I am naïve,
And that I agreed to hold your things,
How could I not notice you had tricks upon your sleeves,
I thought you were a honey bee not a wasp that stings.

I am sorry I am boring,
For not having a dirty sense of humour,
Maybe that's why I am worth ignoring,
Because I am not into all the gossips and rumours.

When I think I am finally over you,
Once a month, the pain comes and visits,
Oh I wish none of this was true,
I wish to feel that I am in home not on the mat in front of it.

~Rawan Ameer (@poetic_author)

I KNOW IT IS LOVE

And I know
it is love,

because I can
hold your hand
for a moment

and never feel cold
for a lifetime..

~Niva Kalita (@feelings_voiced)

AS A GIRL

Just as a toy, as a girl I was told to wind up my neck,
Fearfully, I obeyed.
But the day came when I became a woman,
The day I learned how to wind up words to produce a beautiful melody of words, how to create poetry out of wreck,
I am not a voice to be silenced, I am a voice to be heard by every human.

~Rawan Ameer (@poetic_author)

IF MELANCHOLIA WERE A MAN

If melancholia was a man,
His heart would ache for a woman,
And brain would freeze bleed,
For that mysterious uncommon one,
The girl playing down right there.

Because a heart with hundred spokes can't be precise,
The ring with natural pearl never accurate.
A lambaste over choices never makes anyone stand,
A lost in labyrinth is difficult to path.

So would melancholia know the girl,
And why she's the right choice,
Cause she does not fear gloom,
She runs behind and keeps bloom in her torn pockets for the saddest moments,
That inert virus in her, she's never afraid of it like others,
She's free a believer of freedom.

Melancholia would keep as he knows,
His shadows would never pull her into agony he causes,
She believes flavours of life,
She's not into leaving but holding
She would grab his hand in her's even in the darkest moments,
And lead to the brighter side.

Because the man melancholia knows,
Even her silence gets cacophonies of happiness and laughter,
Her heartful sweets lie deep down to anemones from oceans ,
It swings with those hot-cold currents,
Still keeping up with the lover clownfish.

And that’s the reason why melancholia
is her firm believer,
He unlike for others,
He's still waiting for the only her
To come ,
and clean the cobwebs and dust from the heart that was
lying in the rusty corner of this cosmic world,
And bring melancholia out of the anguish
into a happy place..

~Ajay Sawant (@rumiet.ry)

PERSPECTIVE

I used to think,
I was the sun,
You were my fern.
When I realized,
I was the gardener,
I watered your roots with my tears.

~Lyn Patterson (@poetryntings)

LOVE

When someone fortuitously steals your unsuspecting heart
And simultaneously takes your breath away,
Your heart aches not from sadness or pain,
But from overwhelming desire and constant longing.
It's instant and all consuming,
Love.

~Rosalie Pantzalis (@sserpfl_rn4l)

WE 'LL MEET AGAIN

We'll meet again,
In a land of fairy tales,
With no more worries,
And no more pain.

We'll meet again,
On a joyous ride,
Miles away from the hospital beds,
Admiring the moon seaside.

We'll meet again,
Centuries before death,
In a room full of art discussing,
Van Gogh's life and death.

We'll meet again
Drenched in the rain
In a field
Between life and death.

We'll meet again
When the Earth dies
A natural death
Giving us birth once again.

~Isha Singh (@shhitsish)

BAFFLED BY LOVE

"Chaos in head"
Yet there is calm in her voice

"Heart crying"
Yet there is smile on her face

"Millions of thoughts running inside"
Yet she is composed outside

"A lot to say"
Yet words are not enough to convey.

"Mind is here"
Yet her heart belongs elsewhere

For this is what love does to her
She's alive yet died !

~Niksha Nath (@niksha_justanamateur)

WAITING

Wait.
Keep waiting.
By the bed.
By your mate.
Keep Waiting.
You drop the coin into the lake.
One day your mate is going to wake.
Nowhere to go.
Nowhere to escape.
Let him sleep.
Let him breathe.
People will say anyway.
But you have to find
your own way.
Let him sleep.
Let him breathe.
He's going to wake
One day.
Promise me that,
You won't lose hope.

Miracles happen everyday.
He's going to wake one day.

~Isha Singh (@shhitsish)

TOO LONG

Raindrops on our window-panes,
To me they seem like refugees
of the wild blue yonder.
Helplessly, they stick to what they find first,
right after they are forced to leave.
And we welcome them with our windows closed,
treat them like fallen angels;
for don't we know lucifer? Not at all?
So they stick and they bide
and they sing and they beg,
They mourn like 'decayed-love',
and we pretend not to listen,
like 'moved-on lovers'.
So they stay for too long
and become nothing from something,
What a waste!

~Varun Sharma (@vs.writes)

TILL THE NIGHT

When dew makes love with the pastures
With glittering dictions of the morning,
And sun peeps out scattering all seven shades
To frame all nightly celestials vanish;
Come to me then,
When blossoms blow a scent
And birds mumble your name,
Step on the grass, bare foot
And undress your soul, as you step on me
Confess your musings till the dusk wears away
And moon shines with her twinkle all our way
To make our bodies burn and hands, entwine
And dive deeper into love, as our senses rhyme.

~Subhajit Sahoo (@subhajits_diary)

LOST LETTERS

In the era of e-mails
Her love was a long forgotten
Hand written letter, speaking volumes about
The late night conversations she has with the moon, about you
Preserving the scent of every jasmine that her tresses held
When she awaited you arrival, every noon
They amass the years she spent, making love to your memories
And the tears that her cheeks kissed,
When she couldn’t find your cologne in the air
The love that she shared with you was rare,
Vintage and treasured…

~ Sheetal Bhatta (@letters_inc)

BLINDFOLD

How naive of me
to hold you close
while all you could see
was freckles that the moonlight
failed to hide.
Yet after all this,
How foolish of me
to still write about you
with blurry eyes
and feet entangled in threads
that remind me of your lies.

~ Anasuya Bardhan (@hridmajhhare)

WARRIORS

Let the constellations part away,
From the form, form the discard shape,
Let them obstacle part you and me,
Cause we ain't different,
my love and your heart,
We are the warriors my dear.

Our hearts burn in the sun,
My love let's not take vintage right now,
So let's keep our lips crushing to leak the juice of pain,
Lets make it run,
Filled with passion and moistening essence,
Let the world soak in the vote,
Allow the adamsonian veins shelter us.

Hest the way ignoring the wagons along,
Lets keep our naked shoulders below the lush green,
Under the hollow trunk of shree bodhi,
Lets tame the desires of tendencies,
Together we'll keep the away bemoan wrenched carnal,
And delve our flesh to the earth, the soil,
Cause we are the warriors my dear,
Lets keep our self warriors and shine in the stars,
Lets not hide behind the clouds.

~Ajay Sawant (@rumiet.ry)

WHEN HOPE DISAPPEARED

It's like I'm sinking..
Every tear I've spent in chasing hopes
seem to be evaporating.
I see people out there,
lucky enough to live
and to be able to sigh and kiss
but
I'm dying,
I'm hoping,
I'm dying.
Every now and then I smile
even though I have found many reasons not to.
A Leap of faith is what they call and I've fallen
beyond my heap of fate
I'm hoping,
but I've fallen
and I'm dying.
Here's my cross of faith,
the last gasp of air that I've gathered,
I'm reaching out to hold on
but all my hope have disappeared.
Alas! I hold my breath,
hoping,
until the end of another Storm,
dying
to hope again.

~Aishwayra Rudrappa (@aishwarya.rudrappa.writes)

THE OPTIMIST

I wanted so much
to be the one you wanted.

I longed for a touch
that longed for me too.

I spent my days and nights dreaming,
that i was the one you were dreaming of.

but it was always just me
lying alone in my room

...wanting, longing, dreaming;

repeating, repeating, repeating...

...wanting, longing, dreaming;

repeating, repeating, repeating.

~Elizabeth Brady (@lightofmylifefireofmyloin5)

IF EVER

I never knew anyone,
Until I knew you,
Love? Oh! it pours.
And I know,
I was born to be yours.
If ever, a storm rages against us,
And you feel afraid of falling,
Then don't look down,
Push trouble aside;
And hug me tight, alright?
We've got the keys to the universe
On our mind,
I just want to let you know,
That You are Mine.

~Asmita Mohanty (@asmitaamohantyy)

MAY IT ENDURE

I,
Day and night, here, stand,
In this graveyard, vast.

Leaves,
One by one, they fall,
O'er to my love's tomb.

'Love,
May our love, from now,
Endure to grow, ever-forth.'

~Edwin John A (@e.j.tulik)

LOVE ENGRAVED

Attached so deep
So deep as the roots of trees;
Thousands of years old.
So deep as the wounds of betrayal.
To you, your warmth..

Knotted so strong;
As the genes with our ancestors;
To you, your affections.
You my love,
Engraved souls of your and mine:
To a place of Divinity.
Skins together in an infinite canvas:
Of foreverness.
To the time when, it will end.

~Barsha Kunda (@the_quotes_cafe)

THE STORY UNTOLD!

Still remember the story untold!
The days were of dark thunder cold.
A soft heart, kiddish at the age of six
Unfortunately, the time was fixed!
Loud were the voices,
Screamed right out of the soul,
She cried like a lion's roar,
Left into the dark dirty floor!
Innocence was murdered and body was buried alive,
Memories of the dark still freak out,
In her mind!

~Sneha Wasan (@snehawassan)

DRY WIND

I thought you were the ocean,
And I drowned myself into your love,
But you were the dry wind that came fast and did not stay!

~Akshay Joshi (@mr.thornex)

MUCH AWAITED RAIN!!

Who's there??
I managed to ask with a stern look trying to hide the state of my brain.

Oh hi ! It's me to whom you are well aware,
A cheery voice comes outside the window that is down the lane.

Within no time I realized its none other than my old acquaintance, the rain !

A part of me exclaimed with joy but then some part was there taking hold on the fear and wanted me to sustain,

Baffled being alone I restrained,
Nothing really worked, everything went in vain..

I cried my heart out soaked with the drops of rain,

Promising me that she'll visit me again
The rain went along with my unbearable pain !

~Niksha Nath (@niksha_justanamateur)

SHARE AND HEAL

Let it out , all the emotions,
that you feel.
The ones that have been consuming,
you since.
Making you feel like,
you were the one in the wrong.
Once you share the story ,
the pain you have once felt.
Then only you will be able to look,
past the cards you dealt with.

~Divyanshi Mishra (@wildpoetria)

FOR NOW

I want to touch you
with my fingers in your hair,
my lips pressed to yours
our bodies flush against each other.

But for now
this is enough.

Our souls touching
across the wide oceans,
Through the words
And emotions we share.

For now I am content
with our minds
falling in love.

Maybe some day
there will be more,
it's all I can hope for.

~ Ravisha Singh (@muserofhearts)

TIME AWAITED

His smile remarks his strength,
But eyes speak his grief.
A story longing to reach,
lies embedded in him.

His Visage is not any of those
special kinds,
But truly he has a force too,
positive on his side.

He isn't my love but a person,
with whom I daydream.
A beautiful bond of respect lies in between,
Keeping my soul attached to his.

My love for him is endless,
without any madness.
This paper be a lot more patient,
and carry my legacy of depthless.

But I fear how far will it go.
would I be able to keep?
All that embedded in me
or will it be out leaving me in grief?

~Nistha Goel (@_alikeu_)

WHEN YOU WERE WITH ME

A little rude, a little sweet ,
When you were with me I had all the colours of greet.

When I cry you make me smile ,
You are the one with whom I can walk a thousand mile.

You erased all the memories from my heart which were bitter,
You came in my life to make me feel better.

It was your shoulder on which I kept my head and cried,
The world was against me but you were always by my side .

Just looking into my eyes,
You caught my lies.

I had eyes but no vision to see the world,
But you made me feel how it was pearled.

Your kind nature is the reason I choose you,
My only wish ,my friend,is never to loose you.

You cared for me even after your last breath,
Our friendship did not part away even by death.

You donated your eyes to me so that I could see the world,
But I need to die to see you because you are my world.

~ Maseera (@maseera.arif)

TRUE LOVE

Under the stars,
Leaving all the scars.
Over the valleys,
You and me making all the tallies.
There is a thing I wanted to share,
Your happiness is what I always care.
Don't go away as I have only you,
Together we will prove our love is true.

~Tushar Ranjan Behera (@the_eloquent_philosopher)

WORTH OF LOVE

I'm no more under the famous delusion,
That love cannot be
anything more than pain;
anything other than sadness or
anything selfish.

Love is beautiful,
purer than other emotions.
It’s always giving
expecting nothing in return,
Always sacrificing for happiness.

Love has been defamed for long enough
Let us now remember it's true meaning.
Love is here for us
from the very beginning.

~ Ravisha Singh (@muserofhearts)

FORAGING

my cranium will always keep
protecting the scars on your fragile heart
so don't fear to let the intertwining wires
nurture, bloom and glow
for a moment let me escape into the phosphenes from your eyes
and oblivion about ephemeral incandescence

~i can sense petrichor

Ajay Sawant
(Founder and Editor-in-chief Globalage Poetry)

i know those scars and bruises imprinted all over my
heart that once marked a glory of my worth
that once told the hidden story confined to my heart
now awaits to be traced and cured
for now i see you as a ray of hope bringing much
awaited dawn after a long haul of darkness
setting me free from the anchor of my own infirmities

~ with this i let you be the healer of my wounds

Niksha Nath
(Founder and Editor-in-chief Globalage Poetry)

For more literary work follow us on Instagram
Our Head Page @globalagepoetry
Caption Arm @globalagecaption
Tyro Arm @globalagetyro
Press @globalagepress

GLOBALAGE POETRY
Poetry for Ages